Inspiring
Wome
Every

Plus ... Special Article, Ministry Report and CWR Events Page

CWR

MIX
Paper from
responsible sources
FSC® C015900

LIZ HANSFORD

Liz Hansford lives in Javea on the Costa Blanca, Spain, where her husband, John, is the Pastor of the International Baptist Church. Before moving to Spain she was a frequent contributor to *Thought for the Day* on Radio Ulster, *Pause for Thought* on Radio 2 and *Prayer for the Day* on Radio 4 and a teacher of English. Part of her week is spent in Place4Friendship, an exciting new café outreach to ex-pats, and in discipling new believers. Liz is also involved in evangelism, prayer ministry and writing for both secular and Christian markets. She has four grown-up children and four grandchildren.

CATHY MADAVAN

Cathy Madavan runs Mulberry Communications Consultancy and is involved in writing, communications, PR, and also speaks regularly with Care for the Family and Spring Harvest. Married to Mark, the Senior Minister of Locks Heath Free Church near Southampton, she loves leading worship, planning events and encouraging people to be all that God has designed them to be. Cathy and Mark have two wonderful daughters, and two slightly cheeky chickens! This is her first time writing for *Inspiring Women Every Day* – a task she has loved, although it gave her some sleepless nights worrying about semicolons!

The state of the nation

'Stop doing wrong,
learn to do right!'
(vv.16–17)

When we are comfortably related to God, secure in His special love, part of His people, we can get blasé – especially if everyone around us is the same. But a blast of truth says, 'See yourselves as I see you'.

Isaiah gets right to the heart of things in chapter 1. It's a no holds barred indictment of people who think they know better than God and, in an act of teenage rebellion (v.2), have gone their own way. They are too foolish to understand what they've done (v.3) and God has lost patience. They look the part but there's no substance. They're experts in religion – in fact they do a really good 'Sunday service' – but they have no idea that God has left the building.

God is literally 'fed up' (v.11) with the whole charade. He closes His eyes when they pray (v.15) and He 'cannot bear' their meetings (v.13). Wow! Imagine God saying that of our Sunday worship!

The problem is: there's a disconnect between Sabbath worship and the rest of the week; a mismatch between saying and doing. God wants faith to change how we treat people. We're meant to be honest, not get fixated on profit and money; to notice the needy and do something about it (vv.16–17,21–23).

So, perhaps we need to start this month of studies by singing: 'It's me, it's me, O Lord, standing in the need of prayer.'

And the answer? God says, 'Stop it. Clean up your act.'

Then, if you are 'willing and obedient' (v.19), He will wash away your red-as-crimson sin stains till they're snowy white (v.18). 'Get it settled,' says God. 'Don't leave it any longer. I'm taking how you live seriously!'

For prayer and reflection

Lord, help me to listen to Your Word with intentionality. I don't want to be a casual scanner of Scripture. I want to obey it so that Your blessings are released in my life.

Holy

'Holy, holy, holy
is the LORD
Almighty ...' (v.3)

S moke swirls around the great echoing canopy of the building. The beat of myriad angelic wings criss-crossing the immense space clears the air for a moment and there it is – the train of a vast robe spread over the entire floor, its folds rippling like sunset. In a moment they begin singing – an antiphonal cry that breaks the heart and bows the knee, 'Holy, holy, holy'. The cries crescendo, ringing from the ancient stones, until the whole building shakes. A lone figure stands in terror and awe, then lifts his eyes to where the wearer of the robe sits. Way up, placed beyond where human hands could reach, is a throne, and on it sits the Lord of Hosts, His glory dazzling. Isaiah groans with the gut-wrenching agony of a man who knows that he faces ruin, that he is pitiful and dirty and beyond human hope; that his speech has been the death of him and that everyone he knows has got caught up in ugliness of word and speech that should never have been said.

For prayer and reflection

The altar of sacrifice is glowing, the place where sins could be atoned for. If only! If only! But the distance between holiness and purity and his own filthy heart is too great. He watches, as one of the angelic host hovers over the altar fire then sweeps towards him, carrying a burning coal in golden tongs. Red-hot, searing agony bears down on him. He opens his mouth in a silent scream and in a moment the angel has cauterised his erring lips. 'Forgiven, forgiven!' The words amaze. And in an instant his life is transformed.

Lord, help me to face the effects of my speech. Please forgive me through the atoning sacrifice of Jesus who gave Himself for me. I will go, please send me.

Only when we see what we have been forgiven will we go to serve, whatever the cost!

WEEKEND

Isaiah, man of influence – access all areas

For reflection: Matthew 7:7–12

'… how much more will your Father in heaven give good gifts to those who ask him!' (v.11)

I saiah had access to two important people – the king (in fact a succession of kings) and the King of kings. Jewish tradition suggests that he may have been a cousin of King Uzziah, a position of significant influence.* But no amount of earthly influence compares to being close to the Lord God Almighty. Whether you're a nobody or a somebody, you have the fullest possible access to the King of kings. And you have a world to influence.

Margaret, almost 80, with failing sight, shaking with Parkinson's disease and living in an old people's home was one of the greatest 'nobodies' I have ever known. She had such close personal contact with the King of kings that she changed the world more than most politicians ever do. She knew exactly when to pray and what to pray for, with such accuracy that it would have been uncanny, had I not known that God was speaking directly to her. If Margaret can do it then so can you and I. It simply takes time – building a relationship with the King Himself.

Optional further reading
Genesis 18:20–33; James 4:2–3; 1 John 5:14–15
*See: http://www.free-online-bible-study.org/bible-study-isaiah.html

God **the reliable**

'If you do not stand firm in your faith, you will not stand at all.' (v.9)

How do you know that God is with you? Answer: If you're living in active faith and not hedging your bets with a careful back-up plan – just in case God doesn't come through.

Immanuel, 'God with us', is walking with you when you're the only one believing that God will do it, trusting when all around are suggesting more practical alternatives. Faith and 'God with you' is the same thing. God does not abandon faith-walking people. He may leave to their own devices the 'go it alone' ones – since they prefer to trust human strategies, and so miss out on what God might have done. Or they only get to see it as outsiders, looking on as God unfolds His plan for the trusting minority who decided to risk all on Him, the big faith ones who looked like they were out on a limb.

Ahaz, king of Judah, was tempted to circumvent God's plan with his own schemes and political alliances. Very understandable fear was driving him. In fact, he and his people trembled like 'trees ... shaken by the wind' (v.2). But God said, in effect, 'TRUST ME. Though it looks bad it won't happen. In fact I'm letting you know now that within 65 years your enemies will be shattered (vv.7–8). And I'm going to give you a sign. A virgin (young woman) will have a child and, before he's of mature years, the two kings you are so scared of right now will be facing utter devastation' (v.16).

For us, those ringing words, 'the virgin will conceive' (v.14, NIV 2011) mean Immanuel, Jesus. The words of prophecy had a double meaning – one fulfilled way back in the eighth century BC and the second in the birth of the Messiah. And He is still here – God the reliable – with us.

For prayer and reflection

Father, there's really no choice. I'm going to trust You – even when others go for the supposedly safe, human solution. I'm risking all on You. Committed. Yours. Fully.

Why send **a child?**

Isaiah 9:1–7

'For to us a child is born...' (v.6)

Helpless, hopeless, lost in a maze of confusion, in their despair cursing both God and their weak king, Ahaz (8:21), Judah was a very troubled nation. So desperate were they that they had even consulted mediums (8:19). It felt like stumbling around in the dark, a perpetual black night that never ended in dawn. 'I'll do it my way' had been their approach to life and so God said, 'OK, so be it'. And in judgment He sent the Assyrians sweeping down from the north, overrunning the vulnerable areas of Zebulun and Naphtali (v.1) near the border, pouring over the whole country like a flood reaching up to their necks (8:8).

But God does not judge His people for ever! The people who had 'walked in darkness' would one day see a 'great light' (v.2). Mercy would lift the heavy load that had been on their shoulder (v.4). And a child would do it all. Why send a child? Surely an army is needed to roll back a ferocious, arrogant attacker. But God does things in unexpected ways. No conquering hero, but a child who is also a Counsellor; a Son who is also a Father (v.6).

What do you do when bad turns to worse and there seems to be no hope? When night seems to last forever? When there's no way forward? You turn to a child. An amazing child who will carry you on His shoulders; who will whisper wise words of counsel in your ears; who will father you and bring you a settled peace; who will bring justice to every situation; who knows no limitations and who always does what is right. Don't doubt. 'The passionate commitment of the LORD of Heaven's Armies *will* make this happen' (v.7, NLT, my emphasis).

For prayer and reflection

Lord, I'm on Your shoulders. Safe as a lamb carried home. And Your face is joyful because You found me. How amazing is that!

Real but Invisible

'O upright One, you make the way of the righteous smooth.' (v.7)

So much of what God does for us is unseen. Like the day when Elisha and his servant were protected by a whole army of totally invisible horses and chariots – invisible, that is, to the young servant (2 Kings 6:15–17). In this passage we, the righteous who've trusted in God, are protected by strong city walls. Not actual walls but invisible walls of salvation which keep us in complete safety. We are the only ones who can go through the gates into that place (vv.2–3). And once inside we are secure. When our children were doing the dreaded British 11+ exam which would determine their future schooling, I reminded them that they were amongst the only children in the exam room who were not alone, that they had their invisible heavenly Father by their side. That's true for us too. He is our invisible shield, our protector in every situation. He will not let us come to harm.

But what about those testing situations where we have to wait? Whether you're hovering by the phone or sitting on the edge of your seat in a hospital corridor, God can step in and calm your heart, 'keep [you] in perfect peace' (v.3). You can't pay for it or work it up with effort. But there is something very specific you *can* do. You can choose to consciously focus on Jesus. This is not some kind of mind trick or distraction therapy. It is a promise of God. It is filling our thoughts up with the One who knows the outcome and has it in hand. It is thinking about His power, His willingness to intervene, His good outcome whatever the news, His great purposes for your life, His complete love for you.

Real but invisible!

For prayer and reflection

Lord, I'm coming right now, running through the gate into the safe city of salvation, surrounded by Your protection and love, in absolute peace as I rest in You.

CWR MINISTRY EVENTS

DATE	EVENT	PLACE	PRESENTER(S)
Nov	Christians @ Work	Waverley Abbey House	Beverley Shepherd
Nov	Understanding Yourself, Understanding Others MBTI® Basic (for counselling students)	WAH	Lynn & Andrew Penson
Nov	Deeper Insights into MBTI®	WAH	Lynn & Andrew Penson
-21 Nov	Revelation Bible Discovery Weekend	WAH	Philip Greenslade
-23 Nov	Introduction to Biblical Care and Counselling	Pilgrim Hall	Angie Coombes, Richard Laws & team
Nov	Insight into Depression	PH	Chris Ledger
Nov	How to Help Couples with Troubled Marriages	WAH	Heather & Ian Churchill
Dec	Women's Christmas Celebration	PH	Lynn Penson & Abby Guinness
Dec	The Life and Times of Jesus	WAH	Andy Peck
-27 Dec	Christmas House Party	PH	Steve & Sandra Piggott

ease also pray for students and tutors on our ongoing **BA in Counselling** ogramme at Waverley and Pilgrim Hall and our **Certificate and Diploma of ristian Counselling** and **MA in Integrative Psychotherapy** held at London chool of Theology.

For further details and a full list of CWR's courses, phone **+44 (0)1252 784719**, or visit the CWR website at **www.cwr.org.uk** Pilgrim Hall **www.pilgrimhall.com**

God – **all on His own!**

Isaiah 30:1–21

'[God] rises
to show you
compassion …
blessed are all who
wait for him.' (v.18)

When the forces against you seem impossible what should you do? Worldly wisdom answers: enlist all the help you can get. And make sure those on your side are the ones with expertise, power, ability, skill, cunning, connections, experience and money. In Judah's case: get the Egyptian army on your side and all will be well. 'Remember how big and scary their chariots looked when you were about to cross the Red Sea? A few thousand of them will soon put the Assyrian army to flight!

Sorry, forgot how that story ended. So, it's a big 'No' to the Egyptian horse-led reinforcements then. Anyone got a plan B?

'**God! All on His own?** What, no battalions with banners and charging cavalry? **Rest** (v.15)? You've got to be kidding! **Repent** (v.15)? This is not the time for religious niceties. There's a whacking great Assyrian army coming and they're not here for tea and scones. **Wait** (v.18)? I don't think wait sounds at all like a good idea. **Consult God** and tune in to the Holy Spirit (vv.1–2)? No time for that right now. The sound of hooves in the distance lends a certain urgency to my position! **Listen**, and you'll know what to do (v.21)? Actually, the hoof beats and my heart thumping are kind of drowning out my hearing right now.'

'Others have found it's worked? Really?'

Yes. 'Not by might nor by power, but by my Spirit,' says the LORD Almighty (Zech. 4:6). 'This is what the LORD says to you: "Do not be afraid or discouraged because of this vast army. For the battle is not yours, but God's"' (2 Chron. 20:15). 'Greater is he that is in you than he that is in the world' (1 John 4:4, AV).

For prayer and reflection

Lord, help me to 'Be still, and know' (Psa. 46:10) that You are God. All on Your own You can do all that I need – whatever the apparent odds.

Because you prayed

Isaiah 37:1–8,
14–23, 33–37

'And Hezekiah
prayed to the
LORD ...' (v.15)

When you speak in prayer, God speaks in action. Again and again in Scripture, words make a difference.

The crushing might of the Assyrian army is coming and their leaders taunt the people of Judah, sending them into an absolute flurry of despair. Assyria has already mown down every other town in Judah, and now it's Jerusalem's turn. It was a situation absolutely beyond human hope. All they could hear were the arrogant words of a confident opponent who was sure he was about to decimate them.

Ongoing attack wears you down – especially when it's accompanied by mocking words from those who don't believe and think your God is powerless. Is there any point praying when things are moving towards the end point? The best the people can muster in terms of faith, is a feeble, clutching at straws that 'may be' God will help (v.4) as if to say, 'Isaiah, you pray, we can't muster enough faith to pray ourselves'. But a little faith is better than no faith. If you're facing an 'against the odds' situation, turn your face away from the reality of your awful situation and towards God.

Isaiah's words lift their spirits a little and eventually Hezekiah himself gathers up enough faith to spread out the problem before the Lord. Then, in a jaw dropping miracle, God answers; 185,000 Assyrian soldiers lie dead without the Israelites lifting so much as an arrow. But the heart of the whole episode is in verse 21: 'Because you ... prayed'. God moves when we pray. It's that simple. Our words make a difference. If we don't speak those words, then they can't make any difference. So, however low you feel, get talking to the Lord.

For prayer and reflection

'You do not have because you do not ask ...' 'Ask and you'll get', says God. (James 4:2; Luke 11:9, *The Message*)

WEEKEND

Isaiah the faithful – a long walk in the same direction

For reflection: Hebrews 11:1–3
'By faith Abraham ... obeyed and went, even though he did not know where he was going.' (v.8)

Isaiah prophesied throughout the reign of four kings: Uzziah, Jotham, Ahaz and Hezekiah, steadfastly speaking God's words probably for a period of around fifty years. It was a long, difficult and frequently unpopular ministry. I can imagine Mrs Isaiah saying, 'Can't God give you an easier task? After all, you've been faithful for ages.' But Isaiah kept on keeping on, steadily faithful to the task that God had given him.

Don't run from whatever task God has given you to do. Keep on. The call is easy; the carrying out of it sometimes challenging. When you are tired, keep on. When you are misunderstood, keep on. When you are mistreated, keep on. When it's repetitive and behind the scenes, keep on. Not in dogged determination, gritting your teeth, but in joy and in the power of the Holy Spirit, always listening to His prompting, knowing that He loves faithfulness and that your obedience is a delight to Him. He will make your heart sing as you go – even if, like Abraham, you are unsure of the destination.

Optional further reading
Philippians 3:7–14

Keeping your part of the deal

'The LORD will
save me, and we
will sing ….all the
days of our lives.'
(38:20)

This past summer I faced the possibility of breast cancer. A mammogram led to a scan and then a biopsy. The outcome was my being told I have a 'precursor' of cancer. Benign now but … so I'll have further investigations later.

The whole experience drew me closer to the Lord. I was on holiday as I waited for the result – weeks and weeks here in Spain – and I felt such intimacy with Him that it seemed worth the anxiety. I delighted in His presence and I wanted it to last for ever …

One thing I determined during this time was to speak of how He had kept me and even disciplined me through it, and of how His presence sustains – even when things aren't going well, humanly speaking.

Hezekiah's situation was worse. He was 'at the point of death' (38:1). So he boldly asked God for an extension – and God, wonderful Father that He is, granted Hezekiah's wish. The emotional relief is palpable. From having been curled up in bed crying, the king gets up and starts writing about the experience. 'It was for my benefit' (v.17), he realises. You've forgiven me, you love me. So I'm praising you and from now on, 'I will walk humbly all my years because of this anguish of … soul' (v.15).

But the fame of Hezekiah's recovery spread and a royal prince of Babylon came to see for himself. What an opportunity for Hezekiah to boast in the Lord and what He had done! But instead, Hezekiah gives him the grand tour of his wealth and might, boasting all the while. And God gets forgotten.

So often God gets merely a flickering moment, then I turn back to my self-interest, forgetful that I'm only alive by His will, every single day.

For prayer and reflection

Remembering is important to God. Remembering what He's done will help me stop focusing on myself.

Comfort **at last**

Isaiah 40:1–17

"'Here is your God!" See, the Sovereign LORD comes with power ...' (vv. 9–10)

How do you handle life when things are far from right? Maybe you've faced a time of discipline or emptiness and uncertainty, a time of not sensing Him, a time of grief, or feeling afraid or angry and frustrated, a time when you're simply lost. The simplest answer is to lay yourself open to His word, co-operating with whatever He wants to do. Then you wait. Wait for His words of comfort, for He is a God whose unfailing love will eventually sweep over you, His heart breaking for you despite – or perhaps because of – the path you're on, speaking tender words of reassurance and restoration.

Difficult times are only temporary. He is our 'long-term' God; God who knows our limitations (vv.1–2); God in control; God with a purpose (v.2); God the immense (vv.12–17); God who speaks tenderly (v.2); God who takes us beyond the difficulties of today into the hope of tomorrow (vv.3–5); God who speaks and it happens (v.5); God who, in effect, shouts, 'Just wait till you see what I'm going to do'!

Today's passage was given to God's people before He took them into exile in Babylon. And it was given so that they'd be sustained with hope. He had a purpose in their painful experience. But He would one day bring them back and they needed to hold on to that knowledge – that beyond today was a future and He was not abandoning them. He would come for them in person – not just send blessings but bring them Himself. He is on His way (v.3)! Here He comes in power (v.10)! But don't be afraid for He comes as a shepherd and He'll carry you home, holding you close to His heart (v.11).

For prayer and reflection

Lord, thank You for the comfort Your promises bring. Thank You for Your tenderness. Thank You that one day I will see Your glory revealed and it will all make sense.

Here am I, send someone else!

'Here is my servant, whom I uphold. My chosen one in whom I delight ...' (v.1)

God chose the Israelites, His servant nation, not so they could engage in self-congratulation at being chosen, but so that they would be a light for others. Their purpose was to guide other nations to God, showing them how to relate to and depend on Him, how to be obedient and blessed by Him. They were a prototype, a model.

But instead of being lights, they ended up being disappointments – both deaf and blind to Him (vv.18–19), endlessly, repetitively disobedient and useless as role models. In fact their usual pattern of life says, 'this is how not to do it!' They were like a Christmas toy with no batteries: not going anywhere and not doing anything.

Enter Jesus, the servant of verses 1–7. The obedient servant who would fulfil God's purpose and bring the nations to Him. And God is delighted in Him.

Enter power (v.1) – the power of the Holy Spirit, so that He will steadily and quietly and with gentle encouragement bring about justice and hope (v.4). He does not harangue, but tenderly lifts crushed people who've been battered by life, those whose light is nearly out. He doesn't yell at them and He never gives up on anyone or anything. He is hope for the no-hopers. He is colour and shape for those who have never seen a thing. He cuts ropes and untangles chaos and un-messes minds, so that those hopelessly trapped can step out of whatever entangled them. He is the servant liberator (see Matt. 12: 17–21).

His task is to shine light in every last dark place on earth – exactly the task His people had failed in. It's a new thing (v.9), a 'hope thing' and He's come in person to do it.

Do you know what God's purpose is for your life and are you co-operating with Him in accomplishing it?

Total care package

'... I provide water in the desert and streams in the wasteland ...' (v.20)

Buy travel or car insurance and you can be sure there'll be a few exclusions – 'pre-existing conditions not covered'– you're just too much of a risk. You've lost your 'no claims bonus', got a few penalty points and the result is that your past has pretty much blighted your present.

With God it's totally different. In fact, pre-existing conditions are His speciality. When He's providing the 'cover', He takes care of everything, no extra cost, no naming and shaming.

God's people might have thought He had good reason to turn His back on them. They had messed up so why should He not abandon them. They had no hold on Him, except for one thing – His unfailing love. As He says in verse 4, 'You are precious ... honoured ... I love you.' And that's true of you too. Love keeps God coming after us. '[I] created you ... formed you ... redeemed you ... gave you a name,' says God. 'You are mine' (v.1). His is no passing, flickering interest. It is committed love that has been there from the beginning. It is the kind of love that will see you through tough times, keeping your head above water, wrapping His total protection around you when the fire burns hot. When things are bad the great 'I AM' keeps you.

You are not to be afraid. For, as well as a protected present, He is working on a good future for you. He is doing a new thing. God never stops where He is. He is still 'forming' you, reshaping your world, marking out a way forward, making sure you'll always have what you need (v.19).

He asks for so little in return – that you praise Him and give Him the glory (v.21) – that you respond with a loving, thankful heart.

For prayer and reflection

Do you realise how precious you are?

The obedient **servant**

'I will not forget you! See, I have engraved you on the palms of my hands ...' (vv.15–16)

I f you've ever felt like a servant – 'All I ever seem to do is pick up after you kids!' 'My boss thinks I'm her personal slave.' 'I'm the dogsbody at church; unnoticed and unappreciated,' – then take a look at Jesus the servant. Love kept Him going; a mother love that will not let her children go (v.15); a love so foundational that He's scored your name on His hands so He will never forget you or the task He's been set.

Here, in the second of the four 'servant songs' found in Isaiah (the first one was in chapter 42), we see just a few of His tasks. He has a mouth like a sharp sword (v.2), so He is to speak words of truth that get to the heart of things. He is to reveal God's splendour (v.3), showing us how amazing and wonderful God is. He is a shepherd, lovingly gathering and bringing back those who have strayed (v.5). He is to release captives, leading them home to safety and providing for them as they go (vv.9–12). He has a worldwide task: to be a 'light for the Gentiles,' spreading God's kingdom to the whole world (v.6). Not only will He be a covenant keeper, He will be the covenant itself – the very essence of the agreement with God (v.8).

And with this heavy load of tasks, does much appreciation or encouragement come His way? No! Verse 7 tells us He will be 'despised and abhorred' and there will be times when it will look like failure (v.4). But God has it under control; it 'is in the LORD's hand' (v.4) and He will reward the faithful servant – a reward far better than the accolade of any human being. But the best of all His rewards is us and our thankful, singing grateful hearts!

For prayer and reflection

I am commanded to listen (v.1). As I've listened today to all You, Lord, have done, help me to shout for joy, rejoice and burst into song (v.13).

The Time is Now

During the season of Advent we prepare to celebrate the birth of Jesus, and also remember the promise of His second coming. In *The Time is Now*, the latest of our popular Advent Book series, Amy Orr-Ewing helps us to discern the purposes of God as we see how perfectly His timing worked out in the lives of biblical characters. Let's remind ourselves how God is faithful to fulfil His promises – even when that means waiting for His timing, not our own.

Bible reading: Micah 5:2-4

There are few things as harmful to a relationship as a string of empty promises never fulfilled. But we see from today's reading that God doesn't believe in empty promises. The prophet Micah had received a prophecy of hope against the backdrop of humiliation. Micah was writing in the context of a city under siege in 701 BC. Micah prophesies that Bethlehem, the town of David, will be important again – God will raise up a Messiah from that place.

Hope would rise from the place that Israel's most beloved king, King David, had come from: Bethlehem. 'Bethlehem Ephrathah' means 'a house of bread', promising fruitfulness, not starvation in the future, a longed-for end to the famine of siege. Micah's is a vision of hope and of a delivering king, while things are incredibly bleak all around. God is encouraging His people, and the little town of Bethlehem in particular, to hold on in the difficulties of the time they are in and to wait for the *kairos* event [the appointed moment] – for the Deliverer from Bethlehem to arise.

Micah's prophecy is that hope would take the shape of a ruler. The title here is not 'king' but 'sovereign' or 'ruler'. There will be something different about the new Ruler, and yet He will have royal blood in His veins, from the tribe and the place of Bethlehem. This is a clear messianic prophecy, which Jesus wonderfully fulfils. Micah could hardly have imagined how significant his words would be.

We also see that the Ruler will be as a shepherd to people: 'He will stand and shepherd his flock in the strength of the LORD, in the majesty of the name of the LORD his God' (v.4). This is a hope for care and nurture. In the midst of the loneliness and sorrow of a siege, the prophet looks forward to the time when the Messiah will come and shepherd the people. How wonderful that Jesus called Himself 'the Good Shepherd' and fulfilled this prophecy so completely.

The prophecy of Micah also tells us that the turning point (or *kairos* event) will be a baby being born: 'Therefore Israel will be abandoned until the time when she who is in labour gives birth ...' (v.3).

Even though this prophecy had been given around 701 BC, in a time of desperation for Israel after 700 years – the time comes and *hope is fulfilled*.

Pause to reflect:

Don't give up when times are tough – God doesn't believe in empty promises. There were so many reasons for God's people to despair, so many reasons to believe that things would never get better. After 699 years the Jews could have concluded, 'God has let us down, things will never change', but they would have been wrong. God fulfilled Micah's prophecy, and Jesus, this baby born in Bethlehem, was all that they had been waiting for.

In Trafalgar Square every year there is a Christmas tree which is given by Norway as a thank you to the British people for helping them be liberated during the Second World War. They waited under oppression, and eventually the promise was fulfilled. As a sign of their gratitude they faithfully send a tree to London each Christmas. They remember what was achieved. They remember to say thank you.

Pray:

Thank God for sending Jesus in His perfect timing and ask Him to help you to trust His timing in your life.

The Time is Now
By Amy Orr-Ewing
84-page paperback, 148x210mm
ISBN: 978-1-85345-803-3
£6.99

WEEKEND

Isaiah, fully connected – holding both ends

For reflection: 2 Corinthians 5:16–21
'[He] gave us the ministry of reconciliation.' (v.18)

I t has been said of Isaiah that he had his head and heart in the things of God and his feet solidly on the earth. And that's really the only way to live the Christian life. We are connected at both ends: living godly lives in an alien world, bringing God's thoughts into human situations, speaking God's words as we open our mouths. The starting point is realising that we belong in two places and we must bring the values of one world into the other. We are translators for a society that doesn't speak God's language. We are interpreters of God's ways.

But we must not let go of either end of the rope. And the danger is that one end may slip. We can settle in to this world so much that we stop hearing heaven. Or we can be so focused on the Lord, or churchy things, that we will fail to connect in any meaningful way with this world. We are visibly human, invisibly God's daughters. So let's show more of our invisible selves.

Optional further reading
Philippians 3:17–21; Hebrews 13:11–16

The awfulness of sin

> '... he was
> pierced for our
> transgressions …
> and by his wounds
> we are healed.'
> (v.5)

Philip, aged five, had done something naughty again, so I headed down the hall ready to mete out justice. 'No, mum!' said Nathan, aged nine. 'I'll take his punishment.' I stopped in my tracks. 'That's what Jesus did for us,' I said. So, gently, tentatively, I punished Nathan. But I simply could not bring myself to administer anything like what had been deserved. In fact it made a mockery of the seriousness of what Phil had done and we all knew that the disobedience had not really been dealt with.

The whole world has ripped and torn our relationship with God to shreds. We have stamped our feet and defied Him, constantly disobeyed what He's told us to do, and piled sin upon sin till we're miles away from God. But Jesus says, 'Father, I'll take their punishment.' And the Father says, 'But the punishment must match the crime, for sin is so awful and they must know how dark they have made their world and how serious and terrible it is. It cannot be a cheap thing, without any sense of real justice. As they are now, I will cast them out of my sight, for they are stained beyond recognition.'

'I will take their punishment,' says Jesus.
'You will be pierced, crushed and wounded.'
'I will take their punishment,' says Jesus.
'You will be disfigured and despised and rejected.'
'I will take their punishment,' says Jesus.
'You will die.'
'I will take their punishment,' says Jesus.
'They will find peace and healing if you do.'
'I will carry it all,' says Jesus.
And He did.

Thank You that You did it. That You made the hard choice to set us free by coming into our world and standing where we should have stood. Thank You for love in action.

More

'Enlarge the place
of your tent … do
not hold back …'
(v.2)

Why be satisfied with small numbers or toned down experiences of God or limited expectations of what He will do? Has the past – either your own failure or the low horizons of those around you – made you expect little in the way of blessing?

The truth is God wants multitudes to know Him. He promises significant increase and we are to get ready for it. That means acting in faith now – for the tent was to be stretched *before* the numbers grew. It was a promise to rebellious Israel whom God had turned His back on in anger (v.8) but was now restoring. And it is still how He works. Remember, 'All over the world this gospel is bearing fruit and growing …' (Col. 1:6). 'Be fruitful and multiply', 'go make disciples' is His norm. One day He will rule the entire world. And you are to be part of this successful, overcoming kingdom.

So how can you get from where you are now to that amazing future?

You start with relationship. His heart is full of *chesed* – unfailing love (v.10) – for you. It is a love that *never* lets go, will never abandon, will not go on being angry. If you have strayed from the Lord, remember that 'with deep compassion [He] will bring you back' (v.7).

Having called you, redeemed you and restored you He wants you to stand secure in Him. No more fear, no shame at what you did or said, no disgrace or humiliation. Having dealt with sin He does not keep harping back to it – we do that to ourselves! He wants you to move on. And that means growing, planting, dreaming His big dreams. He is establishing His kingdom and He is doing it through us – you included.

For prayer and reflection

When God deals with the past He does so thoroughly. He holds no grudges, expects no further payment for sin and puts no limits on how close you can get to Him.

Come

'...turn to the LORD, and he will have mercy … he will freely pardon.'
(v.7)

There is nothing small-minded or limited about God. He pardons *freely*, invites *all*, makes agreements which are *everlasting*, loves *faithfully*, thinks the *highest* thoughts, accomplishes *everything* He sets out to do. It's all so, so good. Everything He offers is amazing, yet simple: the best possible life, no stones instead of bread, no scorpions rather than eggs (see Matt. 7:9; Luke 11:12). No spiritual frauds. I have just been reading about holiday accommodation where you are invited to 'enter into the owners' "energy circle" and do Qi Gong under the olive trees'. Why do so many of us scrabble around, for 'what does not satisfy', whether material or spiritual, and may even do us harm? Pseudo spiritual experiences and a home full of things don't bring happiness. God's 'good life' doesn't work that way. What He offers is pure and good and completely free. You just need to 'seek' Him, to ask and to 'turn' (vv.6–7). And, once He has committed to you, it is for ever – a covenant which He will not break (v.3).

Often our thinking is so clouded that we can't see straight. So we have to toss out what we have clung on to as normal and let God's way infiltrate our minds. He sees how things should be, so, aligning our ways with His will bring harmony and satisfaction. Put simply, He thinks differently. No wonder His spoken word changes things (v.11). It is in tune with how the world actually is and it comes from immense power.

When you go His way there is so much joy that it's as if the mountains and hills are singing and the trees are clapping, and so much peace of heart that nothing can destroy it (v.12).

For prayer and reflection

Lord, I'm coming. I want the kind of joy that is found in the simplicity of listening to You and following. Give me Your wine and milk and richest of fare today.

Spending myself

'The LORD will
guide you always;
he will satisfy
your needs in a
sun-scorched
land ...' (v.11)

Why is God not responding? I've prayed, read my Bible, listened to sermons and fasted. What more does He want?

In the Canaanite religion, the underlying belief was that people had to put pressure on the gods in order to make them hand out favours. Man could manipulate god. But the true and living God doesn't operate that way. You can't put a coin in His slot, press the button and get health or a new job or a husband out. God gives. But He gives without pressure or duress or bargaining. He gives freely, profusely, copiously. But he chooses what He gives. He responds to prayer (v.9) and blesses more than we can ask or think – look at the list of good things on offer here: guidance, strength, a flourishing life (v.11), personal restoration or healing, protection on every side, light filling your life (v.8).

But there are terms and conditions, 'then' (vv.8,14), 'if' (vv.9,13). God wants a heart that shares with the poor, fights injustice, cares for family, meets basic human needs and does it quickly – 'when you see' (v.7) indicates a speedy response, an instinctive, spontaneous giving of oneself. We are to 'spend' ourselves (v.10), give our very being.

I ask myself at the end of each day, 'What did I spend myself on today?' And what I spent myself on will be a reflection of my true values, how I'm using up my life. It will show where my heart is. And when my heart is right, God acts.

If you want all these blessings, turn away from thinking about them and instead let your heart catch fire for the needy, give yourself to others and the Father will give Himself to you.

For prayer and reflection

Father, turn my heart away from selfishness and self-absorption. Open my eyes to really see those who are hungry or cold. I want to give myself, not just a few coins.

Radiant reflectors

Isaiah 60:1–22

'Then you will look and be radiant, your heart will throb and swell with joy ...'
(v.5)

N o light, no sun, no moon. A power cut has closed down every electricity sub-station and deep darkness has fallen on the earth. From China's eastern seaboard to California's coast, from Russia's northern reaches to Antarctica the entire world is in deep, overshadowing darkness. But in one place a radiant light shines and so, people from across the globe stumble their way towards it. They are coming to the Light of the world. How do they know that He has come? Well, what happens is that He 'rises upon' us (vv.1–2), 'His glory appears over [us]' (v.2) and as we stand in that radiance we reflect it. Word goes out across the globe that the light is coming both from the Lord and his unlikely little group of despised people (v.15).

The people of the earth are world-weary, needy, without hope, desperate. And the dazzling light draws them like a magnet. So they pour in, carrying the wealth of the nations' (v.11) and the people who served the living God get to be the recipients! The nations bring praise and honour to the Lord (vv.6,9) but as reflectors of His light we share the gifts, a bounty beyond our wildest imaginings.

So finally, the world will be a place of peace and security (v.18), a place of certainty, where God will shine dispelling all darkness. For 'the LORD will be [our] everlasting light' (v.19) and sorrow will be a thing of the past (v.20).

This prophecy is not yet fulfilled, but one day when the New Jerusalem appears and the Lord comes in His radiant splendour, then the whole world will finally realise the truth: Jesus is the Light of the world. Our God reigns!

For prayer and reflection

Am I reflecting the light of the Lord so much that people see Him and come to find out more? Lord, please shine on me, then shine through me.

WEEKEND

Isaiah the poet – get creative

For reflection: Exodus 31:1-1

I can imagine God saying to Isaiah, 'OK, now I've shown you the visions, all I want you to do is put them into words. Make them sing, give them colour and light, make them strong yet tender, shock and persuade. You're the poet – go write.

So Isaiah's words are rhythmical and patterned – though this is often lost in translation – and his imagery is powerful, poetic, strongly visual and original. Look at this portrayal of men confessing their bitterness and hopelessness, 'We all growl like bears, we moan mournfully like doves' (59:11).

When we are creative we reflect the nature of God. He made things – and He made them beautiful, not just utilitarian. He is designer and artist, wordsmith and craftsman, generous with His paint, clever with His words. So celebrate your creativity – be ready to use it just like Bezalel and Oholiab did! Use dance and drama, painting and sculpture, music and song, writing and every kind of craft and skill. Fling yourself into expression, dare to go beyond the norm. Listen to God as you create and see what He says. And be open to new expressions of wonder.

Optional further reading
Isaiah 5:1–7, Isaiah 59:4–11; You may also be inspired by Luci Shaw's poetry collection: *Polishing the Petoskey Stone* (US, Regent College Publishing, 2003); Anneke Kaai & Eugene Peterson *The Psalms – An Artist's Impression* (Piquant, 1999).

Free at last

'He has sent me
to bind up the
brokenhearted, to
proclaim freedom
for the captives ...'
(v.1)

Repentance leads somewhere! Not to doom and gloom, not to eternal navel gazing and woe, but to joy. When we mourn God doesn't want us to stay there. And the mourning of verse 2, while covering all of life's woes and disappointments, primarily means mourning for sin. So having mourned and grieved, God takes us by the hand to stage two: comfort, joy and blessings. He wants us out of the captivity of misery. He wants us to be free from attitudes and circumstances that confine. He wants us to be released from people and places that limit and control.

Jesus spoke a variation of these words 'the year of the Lord's favour' as the opening statement of his ministry in Luke 4:18–19. He is the anointed one of verse 1. For Isaiah it was an as yet unfulfilled dream. (Although it probably also refers to the release of God's people from captivity in Babylon.) For us the dream is a reality. Jesus has come. He came to open, bind up, release, comfort. He was 'sent' (v.1) by the Father, filled completely by the Spirit (John 1:32) and then He put into action God's plan for mankind. God's great 'prison break', His daring raid into the darkness of this world, to rescue us from sin and fear – and ultimately to get us ready for another world.

So we'd better grab hold of the blessings He's bought and brought. Gladness and beauty and praise should be our daily experience.

Don't stay in captivity – whatever it might be. God's favour is upon you. He sees you dressed in a robe of praise and a crown of beauty. And the praise is because He has released you – freed prisoners sing and shout for joy!

For prayer and reflection

Lord, I claim this freedom for myself. Today I'm moving out of despair and dread into that robe of praise You've got for me and I want to fill it out and make it mine.

The judge of all the earth

Isaiah 63:1–14

'It is I, speaking in righteousness, mighty to save.' (v.1)

'See, your Saviour comes!' is the cry of Isaiah 62:11. So the watchmen are on the look out for His arrival. The previous chapters have been full of joy: their light has come (60); God shows His incredible favour (61); He gives them a new name, Hephzibah, meaning 'my delight is in her' (62). So they are eager to see what more will be theirs.

However, what they see now is a little puzzling. There is a figure striding towards them and his clothes look stained, as if he has been treading grapes in the wine press. To their horror he tells them that the red stains are not wine but blood, and that he is angry about sin and has been meting out justice to those who deserve it.

It's a sobering passage and its themes are picked up again in Revelation 14:17–20 and 19:11–16, so we simply have to face the fact that God is Judge as well as Saviour. The two are woven together inextricably, for without a Saviour we would all face the justice of His judgment.

For prayer and reflection

Father, I gladly accept Your salvation today, Your sacrifice for my sin, You standing where I should have stood. The Son of God loved me and gave Himself for me.

But don't be afraid, for He always acts with righteousness and integrity, and He is 'mighty to save' (v.1). Something had to be done for His redeemed ones (apparently a more correct rendering of 'redemption') (v.4) and so He came into the world alone to bring about our salvation and also to judge. What an awful thing He had to do! He, whose heart was so 'distressed' (v.9) by our distress and grieved by our rebellion (v.10). We cannot decide how God should act. His holiness is other than we can comprehend. So we need to shelter under the shadow of His wings, accept His sin-bearing for us, so we can stand completely free from any guilt.

I'm coming **back**

Isaiah
63:15–64:12

'... like the wind our sins sweep us away.' (64:6)

Even though we've messed up would You give us another chance? Remember all You did for us in the past? Despite our wandering ways, You fed us, You guided us, You used Your power on our behalf, You loved us – and we disobeyed and rebelled. What kind of return for all Your goodness was that? So often You might have left us but You never did. Oh, when we rebelled and grieved You, You got angry but we're so thankful Your anger didn't last. We know You want us to return Your love, and we've failed at that more times than we can count.

Today, we want to remind You of every time You blessed us and ask You, 'Was it all for nothing?' We are Your people and through us Your name will be known. So we're asking You to look down (63:15), to return to us (63:17), to tear the heavens open (64:1). There has never been anybody like You – a God who gets involved with us and comes in person (64:3). Unbelievable! A Father who moves into action when we call on Him (64:4). Incredible! But we've experienced it. And we know it can be that way again.

But we've got into trouble – yet again. We got apathetic simply because we couldn't see You at work and we stopped praying (64:7). Bad mistake! But at the end of the day You are our Father (64:8) and our lives are in Your hands. We're in a desert (64:10), we've been through fire (64:11), so we need You like never before. Please bring Your anger to an end. Forgive us. Reinstate us. Speak to us again, just like it was before. We're praying again because we are so lost without You. We are Yours and we never want to be separated from You again.

For prayer and reflection

Father, I've wandered so often and forgotten You. I've been disappointed when You didn't seem to answer and I turned away. Please, in Your mercy, receive me back.

The running **Father**

Isaiah 65:1–16

'My servants will sing out of the joy of their hearts ...' (v.14)

God is an initiative-taking God. A God who says, 'Come, here I am. I know you're not even looking in my direction but nonetheless I'm looking for you.' The story of The Prodigal Son carries the same idea: God looking out for us, checking to see if we are on our way, God running towards us. He is unashamedly a pursuing God. And how good it is to be wanted by Him!

This searching God so wants to be found that He holds out His hands (v.2), a gesture that indicates prayer – He is in effect 'praying' to us, asking us to come. He has spoken to us and even called out (v.12), so we are without excuse. How different are the cults which demand special ceremonies and offerings and the performance of tasks or rituals? But our God is so direct, so straightforward. He comes; we turn to Him, accepted. And all He asks for is the obedient love of our responsive hearts.

Yet many try their own route, playing around with occult practices, crystals, tarot cards, mediums and the whole paraphernalia of a 'spirit' world which they don't understand and cannot control. Here in Isaiah it is 'sacrifices in gardens and burning incense on altars of brick' (v.3), vigils in graveyards (v.4), worshipping Fortune (a Syrian god) and appeasing gods with food and wine (v.11).

So what's the final outcome for each camp? The Lord's servants who follow His way always have plenty, experience joy and in fact become new people, since a new name (v.15) means becoming a different person. In contrast, those who wrap themselves in 'spiritual' practices face nothing but hunger, thirst and death. It's a no-brainer choice really!

For prayer and reflection

It's important not to get caught up in anything displeasing to God, however innocent it might seem. What does God think of horoscopes or colour 'healing' or crystals?

A new start

God just loves doing new things. Think back to His words in 48:6, 'From now on I will tell you of *new* things, of hidden things unknown to you' and 43:19: 'See, I am doing a *new* thing!' (my emphasis). But this time it's on a cosmic scale. God is going to make a new universe. Ironically, He is going to bring the world to an end with an act of creation (v.17)! God doesn't do 'slight improvement' work: He does new birth (John 3:3), new life (Acts 5:20), He needs new wineskins (Luke 5:37), we are new creations (2 Cor. 5:17), He has made a new covenant and there's even a new song (Rev. 5:9).

God will have things the way He always intended them to be, with total peace, absolute security and no sorrow. (Talk of houses, old age and children etc. are pictures taken from everyday life to help us imagine the wonder of life in heaven. They convey a perfect world.) It is above all a place of joy. God shouts it out to us again and again – delight, be glad and rejoice (65:17–19).

So how do I get to be there? Well, it's not by religious observance! He has no eyes for a temple – in fact it's so irrelevant that He can't even see the building (66:1)! But His loving gaze is on those who bend low in their own inadequacy. He prizes humility and a heart that loves to obey. And for those trembling hearts there is a joy-filled future. All our needs will be met (66:11); nobody will make us insecure or threatened (66:12,13); no argument or difficulty will gain entrance (66:12); nothing will stunt our development (66:14). God takes care of our emotions and every need we could ever have imagined. What a good God!

Isaiah 65:17–66:2; 66:10–16

'The former things will not be remembered, nor will they come to mind.' (v.17)

For prayer and reflection

Lord, make me new today. I turn away from the old me and ask You to come in. Please forgive all of my past and give me a new, fresh start in Jesus Christ.

Springtime with CWR

Do you enjoy being with other women and taking time to re-energise your spiritual life? Or perhaps you are looking for a course that will better equip you to serve God and work with others.

This spring time, why not treat yourself to a break away at Waverley Abbey House or Pilgrim Hall? Both beautiful venues, with spacious and tranquil grounds, they are the ideal place to relax, spend time with God, meet other women and be transformed and challenged by enrolling on one of our 'Spring programme' courses.

If a quiet weekend away to take stock and spend time with other women appeals to you, why not join us for our women's weekend at the end of April? So many women tell us how weekends like this have been of great value – refreshing and encouraging them. One guest described Waverley as the 'perfect setting – an oasis of peace and calm'. She went on to say,

'The setting, programme and opportunities for quiet and reflection have helped me to appreciate in a fresh way God's love for me and that He always has my interests at heart.'

Later in the year we will also host the popular Woman to Woman course and a summer women's weekend, both to be held at Pilgrim Hall.

Other courses that are not specifically for women, but which may be attractive to you, are part of CWR's pastoral care and counselling training events. Why not join us for one of these exciting options to expand your knowledge in reaching out to others?

We begin in March with Pastoral Care in the Local Church – designed to help you enable others to grow into their true potential in Christ. Over a period of five days, the CWR Team will envision you with a biblical understanding of pastoral care – helping you to improve your skills in caring for others, showing you how to handle challenging people

Ideal Gifts for Christmas

Advent Products

These 31-day guides cover the whole of December and are great for individual or small-group use.

The Time is Now

As we go about our everyday lives, we can sometimes be unaware of the significant role we are playing in God's redemptive story. Be encouraged by the knowledge that God can work all aspects of your life into His beautiful masterpiece.

By Amy Orr Ewing
96-page paperback, 148x210mm
ISBN: 978-1-85345-803-3
£6.99

Preparing the Way

See how God arranged events for Christ's coming, what was happening at the time of His birth and how people in the Bible were impacted by it, and be prepared for His second arrival in splendour to reign in glory.

By Derek Tidball
84-page paperback, 148x210mm
ISBN: 978-1-85345-613-8
~~£6.99~~ **£4.99 – Save £2.00**

When He Comes

Gain fresh insights into the birth of Jesus and the greatest events the world has ever known, including the second coming of Christ.

By Graham & Molly Dow
84-page paperback, 148x210mm
ISBN: 978-1-85345-566-7
~~£7.50~~ **£5.50 – Save £2.00**

TO ORDER visit www.cwr.org.uk/store or call 01252 784710

Calendars

NEW!

Every Day with Jesus Wall Calendar 2013 - Unchanging Love

Selected Scripture portions, beautiful photographs and inspiring commentary by Selwyn Hughes will remind you throughout the year of how God's grace abounds towards us and sustains us on life's journey.

12-leaf, 210x197mm, spiral-bound calendar
EAN: 5027957001428

£6.99 (inc VAT)

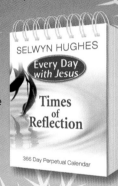

Every Day with Jesus Perpetual Calendar - Times of Reflection

Our flipover desktop-style calendar will encourage you each day with a verse of Scripture and a brief comment from Selwyn Hughes.

372 pages, 109x130mm, self-standing, spiral-bound
ISBN: 978-1-85345-492-9

£7.99 (inc VAT)

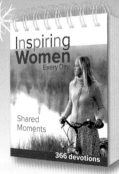

Inspiring Women Every Day Perpetual Calendar - Shared Moments

Based on the award-winning devotional of the same name, this beautiful spiral-bound calendar has a page for every day of the year, each containing a Bible extract and devotional thought.

372 pages, self-standing, spiral-bound, 109x130mm
ISBN: 978-1-85345-493-6

£7.99 (inc VAT)

Or order by post - see order form on last page

Bible-Reading Programmes

NEW!

Cover to Cover Complete –
NIV Edition

Journey through the Bible with 366 daily readings,
arranged in chronological order. Beautiful charts,
maps, illustrations and diagrams plus daily
commentary to help you apply God's Word to your life.

1,600-page hardback with ribbon marker, 140x215mm

ISBN: 978-1-85345-804-0

Special Introductory Offer – until 31 Dec 2012
~~£24.99~~ **£21.99 – Save £3.00**

Encourage your whole church to go on a journey of
discovery with *Cover to Cover Complete – NIV Edition*
visit **www.cwr.org.uk/journey**

Christian Living

I Was Just Wandering
Jeff often describes himself as a Mr Bean of the Christian faith. He has more than his fair share of embarrassing mishaps and laugh-out-loud episodes. In the midst of the laughter and tears, there's a lot to kick-start the heart and mind as well.
By Jeff Lucas
140-page paperback, 210x148mm
ISBN: 978-1-85345-850-7
£8.99

NEW!

NEW!

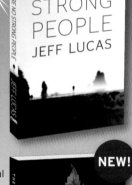

There Are No Strong People
Is it possible to be hugely blessed by God – and still make a mess of your life? In this provocative, breathtakingly honest book based on Samson, Jeff explores some vital principles for living life well.
By Jeff Lucas
234-page paperback, 172x230mm
ISBN: 978-1-85345-624-4
£9.99

The Monster Within book & DVD
In this powerful new autobiography and DVD resource Brian Greenaway gets gritty and personal as he relates the compelling true story of how he turned from a 'monster' to a 'messenger'.
By Brian Greenaway
180-page paperback, 129x197mm
ISBN: 978-1-85345-740-1
£8.99

NEW!

By Brian Greenaway
EAN: 5027957-001404
£10.99 (inc VAT)

Or order by post – see order form on last page

you encounter, and much more.

Next comes our very popular five-day residential course, Introduction to Biblical Care and Counselling. Led by Angie Coombes, Richard Laws and team, it is an ideal way to learn how to put your desire to help others into effective practice. Not only will you be encouraged to reflect on your own life in light of the biblical model presented, you will also be equipped to use the same principles in reaching out to others. This can be a valuable few days as one of our previous participants explains: 'This is a life-changing course which is delivered with passion and honesty. A must for anyone seeking to explore a possible counselling ministry.'

As this issue is being printed, we are already receiving bookings for our courses from women around the world. We do hope that wherever you are, you'll join us this spring and book a place at Waverley or at Pilgrim Hall.

CWR Spring Programme

Pastoral Care in the Local Church
Mon–Fri 11–15 March 2013 (at WAH)

Introduction to Biblical Care and Counselling
Mon–Fri 18–22 March 2013 (at WAH)

Women's Spring Weekend
Fri–Sun 26–28 April 2013 (at WAH)

For more information/to book
call **01252 784719**
or visit **www.cwr.org.uk/training**

WEEKEND

Body Language Reflection: Sitting

For reflection: 2 Samuel 7:18–29

'Then King David went in and sat before the LORD ...' (v.18)

Life is a tapestry of relationships. We are constantly relating with others, communicating and being communicated with. Every day we share information and feelings, exploring those relational connections around us and, ultimately, our lives are shaped by how we communicate and relate with our heavenly Father.

How we communicate is fascinating. This month, whether thinking about work, our role in church, or building our family and friendships, I pray that we will discover new insights for our lives as we explore how David communicated – firstly with himself, then his family, with others in his life and finally with his God. We'll also consider four aspects of David's body language and how we can ourselves use the posture of our bodies to strengthen our faith.

First, let's consider sitting. David sat and poured out his heart-felt prayer. Sitting comfortably, take time to think about the tapestry of relationships in your life: yourself, your family, friends and wider relationships, and your Saviour. Thank God for them all – and pray that you might communicate your love and grace as you think, speak and act each day.

Optional further reading
Psalm 15; Romans 12:9–21

A shepherd's **strength**

1 Samuel
16:10–21

"'There is still the
youngest," Jesse
answered, "but
he is tending the
sheep.'" (v.11)

A round this date each year, kitchen tea
towels escape their drawers to take starring
roles on the heads of shepherds in nativity
plays. These usually comic figures bear very little
resemblance to the young, overlooked, but self-assured
shepherd David. He was eventually brought in from
the fields to meet Samuel, and was described as a fine
looking, brave warrior who spoke well – with harp skills
to boot (v.18)!

I can't help but admire his strength of character.
He had spent years as a belittled sibling, leading
stubborn animals, strengthening his skills, training his
body, battling his fears, and understanding his worth
was found in God and not in how others saw him. This
inner strength equipped him for his amazing journey to
become a shepherd king.

Like David, irrespective of how others see us,
or how challenging our circumstances, we can
accept and enjoy the way God has made us, and
strengthen ourselves with God's help. Like David,
we need to believe in ourselves the way that God
does, understanding that the way we communicate to
ourselves about our life often shapes our future. We
can be so hard on ourselves! There are days I am more
negative about myself than I would be about anybody
else. It is good to stop and notice what you say to the
person you spend all day, every day with – you!

Of course Jesus also described Himself as a shepherd,
and loves His sheep enough to lay down His life for them
(John 10:11–16). Knowing we are unconditionally loved
by *this* Shepherd King should encourage us as we keep
learning to take our thoughts captive.

**For prayer and
reflection**

**Lord, I believe
You believe in me!
Please help me to
take my thoughts
captive, and to
replace words and
feelings of self-
doubt with the
truth from Your
Word. Amen.**

A place of **grace**

Psalm 8

'O LORD, our Lord, how majestic is your name in all the earth!' (v.1)

It can be difficult in our chaotic lives to make space for beauty and stillness to restore us. Certainly the frantic lead up to Christmas is often not the contemplative preparation of our Saviour that I would like! But, as we think more about communicating with ourselves, it is worth acknowledging that we need space for our thoughts to bubble to the surface and our minds to wander past the superficial and the urgent.

Personally, I find nothing more therapeutic than nature, and any time spent surrounded by mountains or next to the sea seems to put my life into perspective and my thoughts in order.

David was embraced by creation as he worked as a shepherd in the valleys around Bethlehem. Nature was his teacher, and rather than it being a retreat from reality, it was where he faced wild animals and elements, and learned to depend on God. Solitude has a way of making us face the challenges and opportunities in our lives – and become stronger in the process.

For prayer and reflection

Creator God, Your world is so beautiful and Your love so faithful. As I calm my mind, lead me to a place of grace where I can be still and know that You are God. Amen.

What a blessing to have David's journal of intimate thoughts in his songs and poetry. Reading his psalms we share those quiet times throughout David's life – as a young man, through battles, through sin and triumph, until old age, where he takes time to express his life in God's presence. Where can *we* find the space to reflect, to listen to our hearts and minds, to be inspired by God and His beauty and truth? Do we value ourselves enough to create quality time communicating our thoughts through journaling, painting or song-writing, reflecting on His creation or meditating on His Word? What would work best for you?

Looking the part

**1 Samuel
17:38–50**

'Then Saul dressed
David in his own
tunic.' (v.38)

oor David really does not look the part. He
is quite comfortable in his shepherd-chic but
Saul is not convinced it's the right outfit for
slaying a giant. So David is dutifully dressed in Saul's
lavish bronze war-wardrobe, but it really isn't working
for him.

What a moment. David is about to move from
obscurity into celebrity, but he isn't thinking about his
reputation, his status, his appearance or his equipment.
He trusts his skill and his heart burns with passion to
defend his God and his nation.

When we are really honest with ourselves, then
we can live life with total authenticity. We don't need
to pretend to be somebody else, the right outfit
won't make us feel more confident, and our lack of
status won't hold us back. How much of what we
construct around ourselves is to hide who we are or to
communicate to others or ourselves that we are stronger
or more significant than we really think we are?

I don't know what giants you've faced this year, or
what looms ahead. You may well feel all you have are a
few pebbles and a heart full of passion for what matters
most to you. But it's when we are most up against it
that the other stuff melts away and who we are and
what we love remain. Fortunately it is in that place of
vulnerable trust that we find the confidence to run like
David towards the challenge, knowing that the battle is
in God's hands.

So let's not worry about looking the part, but focus
on the God who writes the parts, and who knows the
ending. The only thing we need to be is ourselves.

**For prayer and
reflection**

**All-knowing God, I
am sorry for when
I hide behind my
words, deeds or
belongings. Teach
me to be authentic
and to trust You
in every battle.
Amen.**

Faith over facts

1 Samuel 27:1–4

'David thought to himself "... the best thing I can do is to escape to the land of the Philistines."' (v.1)

Today we witness David saying to himself that Saul will kill him and that he should escape to live with the Philistines – of all people. He has enjoyed a series of victories and is clearly at a point where despite the promises from God about him becoming king, and despite the insight of friends and advisors, he is trusting in the facts as he sees them, and in his own wisdom. Consequently, he takes himself and his family into a chapter of compromise and distress.

It's easy to be too self-sufficient isn't it? I often wonder in hindsight why I did not ask friends to pray with me, or spend time with God instead of rushing off with my obviously brilliant solutions to problems. I suppose that involving others sometimes really complicates my plans!

As we pray for those who do not yet know God, navigating their lives by facts and experience alone, we should perhaps also pray for believers, and for the tragedy that sometimes we too settle for listening indiscriminately to our own voice *above* the promises and direction of God. Even when certain facts seem very clear, we do not know the future – only God does.

We ought to check our internal speech and ensure it does not place facts or fear above faith. Of course, we do need to use our common sense (the Bible doesn't advocate ejecting our brains at conversion), but in each challenge we also need to be open to nudges from the Holy Spirit, grateful for the guidance of trusted believers and to be reminded of the promises we have received. Praise God that we are not working out this life alone.

For prayer and reflection

Lord, I thank you that I live my faith as part of the body of Christ with You as our Head. Help me to be open to You and others today. Amen.

Taking **control**

1 Samuel 24:8–13

'May the LORD
judge between
you and me ... but
my hand will not
touch you.' (v.12)

I rather enjoy this season where my normal (half-hearted) healthy disciplines get stashed in the cupboard behind the mince pies and chocolate goodies. It is wise to be able to say 'no' to yourself – something which can be quite difficult. It makes you appreciate the 'I don't mind if I do!' of the festive season so much more!

Being able to control our own impulses and desires is part of becoming more like Christ. David's life is a lesson in how self-control can shape your life. He worked faithfully as a shepherd even when he was secretly anointed as king, and chose not to kill Saul when he had the chance time and again (even though Saul would have killed him in a heartbeat). His God-centred self-discipline was impressive. Sadly, his life later unravels as he lets his self-control slide and his lust and pride get the better of him.

Interestingly, it is when David enjoyed status, success and significance that he was most vulnerable. Perhaps his comfort led to complacency. Maybe under pressure we more readily accept our dependence on God, and display the self-control which is listed as a fruit of the Spirit.

The world may call us to super-size everything, buy more, eat more, watch more and expect more, but we should seek to be guided by the Spirit's whispers and to show self-control where we need to. We can of course enjoy our generous blessings, and by all means tuck into a mince pie, but remembering with grateful hearts that ultimately our fulfilment is found in our Saviour, who surrendered the glory of heaven for a bed of straw.

For prayer and reflection

Lord, I pray that today I would listen for Your whispers through the noise of life. Thank You that it is in surrendering to Your will that I find freedom. Amen.

WEEKEND

Body Language Reflection: Standing

For Reflection: Psalm 18:25–50

'He makes my feet like the feet of a deer; he enables me to stand on the heights.' (v.33)

Research reveals that we communicate far more information non-verbally through body language, facial expression, posture and tone of voice than from the words themselves. You can't help but subconsciously respond when somebody keeps glancing away while talking to you, or when somebody smiles a heartfelt smile. Words are sometimes a small part of what is being communicated. David must be one of the most physical characters in the Bible. His story is punctuated with gesture, action, and vivid emotion. In this psalm (also found in 2 Sam. 22), the sheer physicality of the description expresses the depth of the feeling behind the words. Here David stands and gives thanks for the strength and influence God has given him, and elsewhere we see him standing to survey his surroundings.

This weekend, as you reflect on this incredible psalm of praise, take time to stand somewhere for a moment. In your home, on your street, or overlooking your town; stand as you express your thanks and your dependence on God for all you need.

Optional Extra Reading
2 Samuel 22:1–51; Ephesians 6:10–18

Take Your Church on a Journey of Discovery in 2013!

This year, CWR has republished *Cover to Cover Complete* using, for the first time, the New International Version 2011. The text is divided into manageable daily sections, and charts, maps, illustrations, diagrams and timelines enhance understanding of the Bible and biblical times. Each day ends with a devotional thought written by Selwyn Hughes and Trevor Partridge.

If your church would like to consider going on a 'Journey of Discovery', why not start in 2013? We have a number of resources available to help promote the *Cover to Cover Complete* Bible-reading programme in your church. When you register, you will receive:

- promotional posters
- invitation cards to distribute
- details of special discounts for churches.

Place your order during November and December for a 1 January start. Along with your copies of *Cover to Cover Complete*, you'll receive bookmarks for each individual and all you need to access your church's very own online discussion forum.

Is your church ready for a 'Journey of Discovery'? For more information/to register your church and receive a FREE welcome pack, visit www.cwr.org.uk/journey or call 01252 784782 or email crm@cwr.org.uk

BRAND-NEW EDITION INCORPORATING FULL NIV TEXT

Sibling squabbles

**1 Samuel
17:20–32**

'When Eliab, David's oldest brother, heard him speaking with the men, he burned with anger ...' (v.28)

I remember a particularly long family car journey when, after hours of poking and niggling, my husband quoted to our kids the principle he learned from the film *Bambi* – 'If you can't say anything nice, don't say anything at all!'

We often communicate with our family stripped of the polite layers of padding that we wear for others. And, whether we are sharing intimacy and love, or pain and anger, our tone of voice adds meaning to our words. A simple phrase like 'Have a coffee, why don't you?' can sound quite different depending on whether the tone is gentle and compassionate, or sarcastic and clipped!

This week we listen in as David communicates with his family, starting with a lunch delivery to his brothers, where he asks about tackling Goliath. His oldest brother Eliab (possibly displaying a chip on his shoulder after being bypassed for anointing by Samuel) gives him a real verbal beating. You can hear Eliab's humiliating tone of voice as he asks David where he left 'those few sheep', and his aggression as he accuses him of being conceited and wicked.

Being put down by siblings, family members or those in our Christian family can be totally demoralising. They can push buttons nobody else even knows about. David wisely turned away. We all have to pick our battles – and on this occasion he chose to fight the enemy, not his brother. Imagine if he hadn't. We need great discernment about which battles within the family need to be tackled, and when they need to be faced. God may have other challenges for us to focus on, which could, as with David, change our future forever.

For prayer and reflection

Heavenly Father, help me to forgive where words have wounded me. I pray that the words I speak, and the way I speak them would build people up today. Amen.

Watch **what you watch!**

'The woman was very beautiful, and David sent someone to find out about her.'
(vv.2–3)

'Tis the season to be jolly (and mercilessly bombarded with messages to consume as if we don't have to pay for it in January!) Fa la la la la, la la la la'! It really does seem impossible to escape the lure of the festive adverts which communicate so creatively and powerfully to us. We unwittingly absorb the messages to desire shiny new products and, if we do not watch what we watch, then what we see can prove too seductive to resist. Temptation, even of the most destructive kind, can begin with a glance.

David, a passionate and powerful man, should have 'watched' what he watched. His life is redirected as he takes a second look at the beautiful Bathsheba bathing. His eyes linger as she washes herself, and he wants her, willing to 'buy now and pay later' as it were. David should have counted the cost to his soul and simply looked away, but he chose not to, with disastrous consequences. Bathsheba may have later become his wife (after her husband was dealt with), but this relationship is more about possession and reputation than love.

David's relationships with his many wives and concubines are a stark insight into a culture where women were treated more as commodities than people with rights; but even so, this story is one of David's lowest points. What a contrast he is to the young man of David's heritage, who sacrificed his own dignity to unconditionally love the young and pregnant Mary – a girl whom he had resisted ever sleeping with. Joseph is a moving and counter-cultural reminder that seeing, wanting and getting will always be less fulfilling than giving, sharing and loving.

For prayer and reflection

Lord, help me be aware of what I see, watch and focus my thoughts upon. Today, I resolve to be captivated first and foremost by You and Your Word. Amen.

A wife's **wisdom**

1 Samuel 25:14–39

'David said to Abigail, "Praise be to the LORD, ... who has sent you today to meet me."' (v.32)

In the midst of David becoming overwhelmed with frustration and anger, we meet a remarkable woman. Abigail has got it all going on! As she defuses the potentially explosive situation between David and her tyrant husband, she displays intelligence, logic, loyalty, grace, creativity, diplomacy, tact, planning, wisdom and leadership. *And* we are told that she was beautiful. Wow – what a woman! It is not a surprise that when her husband, Nabal, dies of the shock of what she has accomplished, David takes her to be his wife.

I can't help feeling a bit in awe of Abigail. But note – it is so easy to look up to others and inadvertently put ourselves down in the process. If we are not careful, comparing ourselves to our heroes can lead us to try and be something we are not. I remember a few years ago feeling determined to be Supermum/Super-Pastor's wife for a while, and almost killing myself in the process. My resolutions ended fairly abruptly when I caught my young daughter telling the family we had invited for dinner that they would know when the meal was ready, as the smoke alarm would go off! I kid you not.

But while we cannot and will not ever be anybody else, we can all learn from Abigail's approach in this passage. How can we, like her, navigate our challenges with similar creativity, grace and wisdom? How can we be people who bring peace where there is tension? How can we use our words, skills and personality so that God's will be done? God wants to use you and me today, to bring peace and unity to those we meet. What a calling!

For prayer and reflection

Heavenly Father, I thank You that You have made me unique. I pray that where there is conflict, I will reflect You, and be a channel of Your peace and wisdom. Amen.

A **passionate** parent

**2 Samuel
13:23–33**

'Absalom has
struck down all
the king's sons; not
one of them is left.'
(v.30)

I was once told that your greatest strength can also be your greatest weakness – it's like it has a flip-side, which can sometimes be our character blind spot. If that is so, then David's biggest strength and his biggest weakness was his passion. Passion defined his life – he fought battles to the bitter end, he poured out his heart to God in song, and he led with courage. But passion without self-discipline can be a disaster, and David's passion also led to him becoming a parent to at least twenty-one named children from many mothers, with heart-breaking consequences.

Having so many children would be a challenge for anybody – I sometimes struggle to stay in control of just two and our pets (my children like to remind me that I am the mother that once gave 'time-out' to a goldfish for bullying the other fish by putting him in a bag of water inside the tank – harsh I know!) But David's ever expanding household spiralled seriously out of control, culminating in rape, murder and challenges to his throne.

His passion was impressive, but the flip-side was painful as he failed to moderate that passion, to discipline his family or to adequately deal with the consequences of his actions. What would our strengths and matching blind spots be? I may be really self-motivated but the flip-side is that I wear myself out, doing too many things on my own. What about you? Could being persistent be your strength and weakness? Being loyal? Sensitive? May God help us to be grateful for our strengths, and to humbly ask for His help where we need His wisdom.

For prayer and reflection

Ponder your strengths and explore any possible flip-sides. Lord, help me to be strong for You, and to be wise about my weaknesses as I serve others today. Amen.

Leaving a **legacy of love**

1 Chronicles
28:2–21

'And you, my
son Solomon,
acknowledge the
God of your father,
and serve him with
... devotion ...' (v.9)

Having established yesterday that David may not merit 'Dad of the year', this verse reminds us that at heart he will always be a God-focused man who is open to learning from his mistakes. As an elderly king, his final instructions to his son Solomon (born out of his relationship with Bathsheba) are moving and powerful.

Have you ever had to accept that your dreams may not be fulfilled? God said 'no' to David's dream of building the Temple of God, and David had the grace to accept it. So, in spite of his disappointment, he did what he *could* do – he prepared plans for Solomon, with the benefit of years of wisdom and experience, and spoke words of encouragement and spiritual insight to his son – the new king. You can taste the depth of emotion and meaning conveyed in these moments.

Later, also passing on a legacy of love, Mary and Joseph, with far humbler experiences, nurtured and encouraged their son as He fulfilled His calling to be a king of another kind. Who can guess the value of the comfort and encouragement that Jesus received from them as He rebuilt the kingdom of God in ways they could never have imagined?

We all need those people who will invest in us. And in turn, what could be more fulfilling than helping others to reach their potential? Perhaps today we could pause and thank those who have encouraged us, and then ask God to remind us who we influence each day – and resolve again to do everything we can to communicate with words, actions and time, our love and commitment to them. We can all leave a legacy of love.

**For prayer and
reflection**

**Thank You, Lord,
for those people
who have left a
legacy of love in
my life. Help me
to pass it on, as
I encourage and
love others in Your
name. Amen.**

Have a digital Christmas!

Searching for that perfect Christmas present that will be more meaningful than bubble bath or socks? Know any relatives or friends who have been given Kindles or iPads this year and are avid eBook fans? Or, perhaps you've bought an e-reading device as a gift for someone this Christmas, and are looking for the perfect book to download onto it to get them started?

CWR have invested time and resources to widen the range of titles available in digital formats. You can now purchase daily notes, teaching material, books for women, books for men, plus many other incredible reads, including *Inspiring Women Every Day* notes, and the recently published book *Woman to Woman* – all available instantly to download and start reading.

So don't feel confined to filling those e-readers with novels that only last a few days – browse our online store and find books that will bring life-changing words to last a lifetime.

www.cwr.org.uk/store

WEEKEND

Body Language Reflection: Dancing

For reflection: 2 Samuel 6:1–22

'David, wearing a linen ephod, danced before the LORD with all his might ...' (v.14)

I may be allergic to computer dance games. I boogie away, throwing some shapes on the lounge floor like Kylie Minogue, and then the screen plays back footage of me looking more like Mr Bean. Not so encouraging. But it's true that expressing ourselves through dance, or watching the grace and power of a professional dancer can release and communicate profound thoughts and emotions.

David felt such joy about the ark of the Lord entering Jerusalem that his body simply could not hold back. Despite his wife Michal's cutting sarcasm, David was less worried about being dignified than being abandoned to God.

Pause to read one of the psalms below where David again expresses himself through dance. How does it make you feel? Excited? Liberated? Slightly uncomfortable? How do you express your praise with *your* body? If you feel comfortable, put on a worship song and express yourself through dance! Alternatively watch a professional dance on the internet and enjoy reflecting on how the body expresses emotion.*

Optional Extra Reading
Psalm 30; Psalm 150

*I particularly recommend 'Fix me Jesus' – Revelations by Alvin Ailey: http://www.youtube.com/watch?v=4CXk1mQVCgI

The leader's **anointing**

1 Samuel 16:1–7

'Man looks at
the outward
appearance, but
the LORD looks at
the heart.' (v.7)

Recently, my Dad discovered a letter that was written to my parents when I was 17. It was in the familiar handwriting of my music teacher who had taken me to an audition at a music college, and wanted to express to my family the potential that he and they had seen in me. Reading those words brought back a tidal wave of emotion including gratitude that he had developed in me what I may not have ever seen for myself.

Similarly, this week as we look at the relationships David had beyond his family, we cannot overestimate the power of Samuel's relationship with David. This respected spiritual leader's words brought a totally new perspective to this young shepherd and his family – he saw David's God-given potential, and anointed him for his future.

Samuel, as he deals with Saul and David throughout his life, shows a dependence on God's guidance and courage to follow God's promptings. A respected and godly prophet, he listened to God, and saw David's heart. In turn, David trusted him, humbly submitting to his wise counsel and spiritual leadership. Thank God for those in authority over us who listen to God, who see our hearts and guide us to become all that God has designed us to be. Thank God for the times we have listened and followed the path they have showed us, a path that we may have missed ourselves. In an increasingly individualistic world, we are wise to remain open to the guidance of those godly men and women who teach, lead and mentor us, and to treasure our relationship with them.

For prayer and reflection

Lord, I pray today for those in spiritual leadership in my own church and across the world. I pray You will continue to raise up leaders of integrity and insight. Amen.

The king's **opposition**

**1 Samuel
23:15–25**

'... if he is in the
area, I will track
him down among
all the clans of
Judah.' (v.23)

Unsurprisingly, Herod does not take a leading role in your average primary school nativity play. I like to imagine that if he did, he would be played as a kind of Bond villain, stroking his sinister cat, whilst menacingly announcing his intent to kill all the young boys in the land – in order to wipe out the infant child from Bethlehem who is destined to be king.

Herod's instinct for self-preservation was much the same as the earlier King Saul's – who also relentlessly sought out a young threat to his throne born in Bethlehem. David's relationship with Saul is complex, with Saul constantly sending mixed messages to his nemesis. One minute, David is playing the harp for him, the next he is running for his life. Other times, Saul admits his wickedness as David repeatedly spares him from death, but then he resumes his hunt, blinded by his insecurity. David though, somehow, never loses his respect and even love for the man who persecutes him so mercilessly.

**For prayer and
reflection**

But at the close of play, neither Herod nor Saul could stand in the way of God's anointed king, though neither David nor Jesus took their opportunities to overthrow the kingdom and authorities that constantly oppressed them. Jesus may not have ever lived the life of power and prestige that David did, but like His distant ancestor, He won the battle in the end – this time gloriously returning to the throne of heaven, and reigning for all eternity. Praise God that this baby from Bethlehem is also the King of Kings, and is still establishing His kingdom through us on earth today.

**Magnificent Lord
Jesus, Yours is
the kingdom, the
power, and the
authority, forever
and ever. I pray
You will rule in
my heart and in
my life each day.
Amen.**

A friend's **faithfulness**

I remember going for a spa day with a really good friend of mine a few years back. Whilst waiting for our mud treatment, the spa staff gave us both some paper underwear to wear – but to wear without anything else on at all! My friend and I looked at each other, both thinking, 'I really like you, but do I really want to know you *this* intimately?!'

Truthfully, intimate friendships are rare and precious. Most of us will not be blessed with more than a handful of truly deep relationships to share our lives with. And without a doubt, the relationship between Jonathan and David is one of the Bible's most beautiful pictures of friendship, mutual respect and love.

We read later in this passage (v.41) that when Jonathan realised his own father was planning to kill his friend, he fell on his face and they embraced and wept together. He repeatedly spoke well of David, standing up to his father, and shows no sign of envy or jealousy, which is remarkable since he might have been the heir apparent, and could well have resented this shepherd warrior plundering his birthright.

God knew that David needed an intimate friend who would do anything for him, and David loved Jonathan and honoured his family in his old age. We all need those deep connections which are the antidote to loneliness. We all need to be able to call on people who give us the benefit of the doubt, who listen and cry and celebrate with us. And we all need people who in turn allow us to love them back, welcoming us to make ourselves at home in their lives.

1 Samuel 20:1–11

'Jonathan said to David, "Whatever you want me to do, I'll do for you."'
(v.4)

For prayer and reflection

Thank You, God, for the gift of friendship. I lift my friends up to You today and ask for Your blessing and presence to fill their lives. In Jesus' name, Amen.

The comfort of cave-dwellers

'All those who were in distress or in debt or discontented gathered around him ...' (v.2)

Have you ever wanted to run away and hide somewhere? Or felt so overwhelmed and submerged by despair that you didn't want to see anybody at all? Well, if so, you have experienced your own cave like David, who, in Psalm 142, pours out his desperation and reveals how alone and afraid he feels at this time. Even in these circumstances, it is humbling to see how David declares his dependence on God who is always his refuge.

Then, in that dark cave of escape and retreat, God shines a light. David's family, followed by all kinds of disgruntled strangers turn up, and before you know it, the situation is transformed; this unlikely crowd become David's loyal army – later described as his mighty men (2 Sam. 23:8–39) – and the cave becomes a buzzing military headquarters.

Who would have thought that in that place of weakness and vulnerability God would reshape and reboot David's future? Of course, David was a skilled and charismatic leader and could turn any rag-tag group into warriors and strategists, but it still reminds us that God's only required raw material is utter dependency upon Him. Sadly, sometimes it is only when we are in a cave that we do utterly depend on Him, and see the potential waiting to be unlocked in those around us – whom society or we ourselves may otherwise have overlooked. David's cave reminds us that it is in darkness that God can shine His hope the brightest, and that God will meet us there – turning our despair into courage again as we trust in Him, and discover who around us we can really depend upon.

For prayer and reflection

Merciful heavenly Father, thank You that You meet us in our dark places, and shine Your hope into the shadows of our hearts. Help me to trust You for the future. Amen.

Facing the **truth**

2 Samuel 12:1–13

'Then David said to Nathan, "I have sinned against the LORD."' (v.13)

Last year my husband and I experienced one of the most painful chapters of our lives. We had noticed for some time that a close friend was struggling in his faith, and becoming detached from those around him. We knew there were pressures in his life, but nothing seemed to explain his distance. Eventually, despite repeated opportunities to share, his life and his marriage collapsed, and he left his wonderful wife, his faith and his community to begin life with a new partner. We have never known anything like the pain and devastation that emerged as we challenged and supported him to try and make the right choices.

It takes huge courage and personal investment to be prepared to be a Nathan. Nathan knew David very well, and chose his approach carefully and wisely. He also knew that under the law, adultery or murder resulted in death, and David had committed both. What God-given wisdom and tact he displayed in his communication as he confronted the king!

But then came David's incredible response: confession, repentance and utter remorse. By His grace, God removed the death sentence from him, but the devastating consequences caused David to fast, weep, pray and write psalms like Psalm 51, submitting himself totally to God.

Our sin really messes up our relationships with others and with our Creator, and we all need Nathans in our lives, who help us to face the truth about ourselves, in big ways and small. Also, we could all do with cultivating an open and receptive heart like David's. Praise God that through Jesus we find forgiveness and restoration as we humble ourselves in His presence.

For prayer and reflection

Lord, help me to be wise and courageous like Nathan when I need to be, and to keep a receptive and repentant heart towards You. Thank You for Your forgiveness. Amen.

WEEKEND

Body Language Reflection: Bowing

For reflection: 1 Kings 1:32–48
'And the king bowed in worship on his bed ...' (v.47)

Picture the scene: David, now an elderly man, was bowed in worship on his bed in the royal palace to honour and respect the new king. And as he bowed, this physical act ushered in the next chapter of Israel's journey with God.

Fast forward about a thousand years, and another king was making His entrance, and an assortment of shepherds and wise travellers also came and bowed before Him – but not in a palace this time, just a stable. This king was born to turn the world's understanding of greatness, power, justice, forgiveness and mercy upside down. And as they bowed, another chapter of God's relationship with His people was being written.

Fast forward again, and if you are physically able, take a moment to bow before your King this Christmas. As you honour Him with your body, mind, soul and strength, remember that He is still writing His story of love in and through you, and came in order to restore your relationship with God and give you life in all its fullness (see John 10:10).

Optional Extra Reading
Matthew 2:1–11; Philippians 2:5–11

JAN/FEB 2013

January

GOD, THE PLANTER AND HARVESTER
AMY BOUCHER PYE

February

RUTH: UNDER THE SHADOW OF GOD'S WINGS
CHRISTINE ORME

In **January**, Amy Boucher Pye explores God's role in our lives as the Planter and Harvester, challenging us to root ourselves in Him throughout the varying seasons of life.

In **February**, Christine Orme recounts the timeless tale of Ruth, inviting us to draw parallels between her situation and our own, and to trust in the overarching sovereignty of God.

Please note that from the Jan/Feb 2013 issue, the price per issue will be £2.95. Obtain your copy from CWR, Christian bookshops or your National Distributor. If you would like to take out a subscription, see the order form at the back of these notes.

Also available as ebook/esubscription

Praying **from the heart**

Psalm 145

'The LORD is gracious and compassionate, slow to anger and rich in love.' (v.8)

Recently, some visiting friends were laughing at my mountain of lists. I like to write lists. Okay, I love to write lists. In fact, I'll admit it, it's bordering on an addiction! I actually have a list of my lists and notebooks for each area of lists. It's embarrassing. And Christmas in my house is basically a collection of lists: the kids' wish lists, card lists, presents lists, thank-you lists and food lists. Is anybody with me?

As this week we learn more about how David communicated and related with God, I have to remind myself that spending time with God is not something on a to-do list, but something which should permeate my life. Prayer particularly can become like a shopping list of things we think we need, or a catalogue of names and places which we want to remember to lift before God. Now of course, it is no bad thing to be proactive about prayer, to have reminders, or to use a system to help us to pray – we should prioritise our time and energy to communicate with God. But prayer is so much more than just a good discipline.

Who could fail to be inspired by the prayers of David, which were so honest, so heart-felt and so consistently full of truth about God, that we sense his connection with his Maker whenever we eavesdrop on him praying throughout his life? So, let's put aside the lists for a few minutes, even on this busy day, and have a heart to heart with our Lord. He is always listening, and will speak His whispers through His Spirit as we wait on Him.

For prayer and reflection

Lord, we thank You that through Your Son, we can come into Your presence and talk with You. Hear our prayers of praise and petition this Christmas Eve. Amen.

Servant-hearted living

Philippians 2:1–11

'[He] made himself nothing, taking the very nature of a servant, being made in human likeness.' (v.7)

'Joy to the world, the Lord has come! Let earth receive her King!' It's a magnificent mystery, isn't it? The Word who spoke light and life into our solar system, who artfully sculpted our planet, became the Word incarnate, living amongst us, speaking life and light into our lives. Jesus, because of His love for us, exchanged the majesty of heaven for the meekness of a stable, living a life of obedience, even to death on a cross.

Nobody, in our success-orientated culture, would ever conceive of a powerful person surrendering himself to become a servant; it seems so unlikely. But Jesus constantly modelled His humility before God, always doing what His Father had asked Him, serving those who nobody else would want to serve, and loving with an indiscriminate love.

During David's life we see the same desire to serve and surrender to God, whether in a field with sheep, in a cave with misfits, questioning God about his military manoeuvres, or even sacrificing his dreams to build the Lord a temple. His ambition remained for people to see the glory of the great and faithful God he served, and for Israel to be a light to the nations.

What wonderful examples for us to consider today as we celebrate. What a perfect opportunity as we unwrap our presents and enjoy our festive traditions, to be grateful for the gift of life that Jesus has unwrapped for us. On this special day, let's affirm again – it is God we serve, and others we serve in His name; putting aside our own selfish desires we will allow the Spirit to give birth in us today in new and wonderful ways.

For prayer and reflection

Dear Lord Jesus, thank You for Your birth, life and death. I pray I would be inspired again to serve as You serve, and to love as You love. Be born in me again today. Amen.

A heart of **worship**

2 Samuel
24:18–24

'... I will not
sacrifice to the
LORD my God
burnt offerings
that cost me
nothing.' (v.24)

We have a corner of our house stuffed with musical instruments. There are cornets, trumpets, percussion, a piano, guitars, a banjo, my beloved accordion (I keep telling everybody it is cool, and one day they will believe me), and you might even find the odd recorder or kazoo. I really do praise God for music. It is incredible when you consider the physics of notes and scales, how such emotion, diversity and power can be communicated through melody and harmony.

I love being part of our church worship team, spending time with them, singing and playing music for God together, and sharing in worship with our church. But even so, worshipping God is not always easy, and there are times when my soul is weary, or my body is tired, when it can be exhausting and costly to offer myself up to the Lord, even though I know His presence will refresh me.

David clearly met with God as he played on his harp, and wrote the melodies and words found in his psalms. But more significantly, in this reading we witness him refusing to offer a sacrifice to God which had cost others but not himself. David's heart's desire was to honour and worship God in all kinds of circumstances – with all the strength, skill and creativity he had been given.

What a great reminder to us, that we should desire to seek, love and worship God first, rather than waiting for when we're feeling strong enough. It may cost us more, but we are blessed when we spend time in the presence of the Lord who will in turn strengthen and equip us for all the good things He has planned.

For prayer and reflection

Lord, I worship You today, and praise You for Your power, grace and love. I lift up my heart and voice to You, and thank You that You always walk with me. Amen.

Finding **our strength**

1 Samuel 30:1–10

'But David found strength in the LORD his God.'
(v.6)

This chapter represents a bleak moment for David. He and his men returned to their town to find it an empty wasteland, destroyed by fire, the women and children taken captive. The text tells us that they wept until they had no tears left, and his men, feeling bitter with recrimination, were mutinous as a result. David was unsurprisingly distressed. This would definitely qualify as a bad day.

Very few of us can imagine losing everything in this way, but each of us will have experienced loss, humiliation or grief that leaves us crying until we have no strength left. Where do we turn when there is nowhere left to turn? David with his divine dream in tatters, turned to God, and found his strength and encouragement in Him. We are not told how he found his strength in God, or what took place exactly, but we do know that David moved from despair to determination after that encounter with the Lord.

You simply never know what you are going to have to cope with, until you have to. We have had to deal with my husband's sight degenerating to almost nothing from early into our marriage, and people often say to me that they do not know how we cope. Yet I see others living with illness, disability, unemployment, heartache or grief and I wonder how I would possibly endure those circumstances. But, just because life can be harsh, does not mean that God is. Learning to go and find our strength in Him, finding His courage to move forwards is one of the most profound things we can do, and we can be encouraged that David did the same.

For prayer and reflection

Thank You, Lord, that Your grace is sufficient for us, and Your power is made perfect in our weakness (2 Cor. 12:9). Help me to find my strength and purpose in You. Amen.

Famous last words

2 Samuel 23:1–7

'Has he not made with me an everlasting covenant, arranged and secured in every part?' (v.5)

I always chuckle when I read that the comedian Spike Milligan wanted the words on his tombstone to say 'I told you I was ill!'* What an epitaph! It is fascinating to read how people want to be remembered, including their last spoken words before passing away. Morbid it may be, but it gives an insight into their state of mind as they reflected upon their lives.

Perhaps some of the saddest last words were those of the famous artist Leonardo da Vinci, which are widely recorded as being 'I have offended God and mankind because my work did not reach the quality it should have.'** This is the man who painted *The Last Supper* and numerous other moments of Jesus' life, but who felt disappointed in his work (and perhaps his life), feeling that he had not adequately reflected the glory of the God he had portrayed so many times on canvas.

David's final words could not be more of a contrast. They speak with a confident assurance about how his life had God's hallmark on it, and how God had provided for him and protected him. He had, as Paul would say, run a good race, and had not faltered in his faith, persevering until the finish line. In fact, throughout his life, whether as a shepherd, while on the run from Saul, or managing his kingdom, David regularly kept re-aligning himself with God, trusting in His faithfulness during times of trial or triumph. What a challenge for us – to consider how we can encourage ourselves and those around us to persevere in our faith as David did, reflecting God's goodness until our very last words are spoken.

For prayer and reflection

Heavenly Father, I long for my life to speak about Your faithfulness to me, and I choose to keep pressing forwards each day, seeking to be faithful to You. Amen.

*Miligan: http://www.phrases.org.uk/quotes/last-words/spike-milligan.html
**da Vinci: http://bytesdaily.blogspot.co.uk/2011/11/last-words-leonardo-da-vinci.html

WEEKEND

Body Language Reflection: Pouring

For reflection: 2 Samuel 23:13–17

These mighty men; they had put their lives at risk to fetch some water for David. And what did he do? He poured it out before the Lord, sacrificing the water to God rather than drink from a cup which could have cost them everything.

Mark 14:1–9

This brazen woman; she had put her reputation on the line to bring this perfume to Jesus. And what did He do? He allowed her to pour it out over Him, ceremonially preparing Him for a week that would cost Him His life.

Mark 14:22–25

This Servant Saviour; He invited His friends for a Passover celebration. But then what did He do? He described the wine as His blood that would be poured out for many, and they drank with no idea of the cost involved.

Titus 3:4–7

This generous God; He washes us through Jesus' blood but doesn't want us to live an empty life. So what does He do? He pours out His Spirit, so that we are not only justified by grace, but full of the hope of eternity.

A life **devoted to God**

'... I have found David ... a man after my own heart ...' (v.22)

This may be the most widely known description about David found in the Bible. We read these words in 1 Samuel 13:14, but also here, as Paul recounts the way that God has guided and led His people throughout history. Unlike David, nobody else in Paul's account receives an accolade about their character – and it is a pretty incredible thing to be described by God and by your ancestors as somebody who is after God's own heart.

As we draw to the end of our journey of thinking about how David related and communicated with himself, his family, other people and his God, we should feel encouraged that it is possible to live a life with disasters and victories, moments of sin and moments of courage, and *still* be a person who is devoted to God. David was an imperfect man seeking to follow a perfect God with all of his heart, soul, mind and strength.

Each of us who live in the light of the cross can rely on the Holy Spirit as our guide and counsellor, as we navigate our relationships, communicating with ourselves, others and of course with God. What an indescribable privilege to be able to live life with our Creator, seeking His direction for the plans and purposes He has for us! Paul could never have imagined how God would continue to develop His story with His people, and it is exciting to think that God still has wonderful plans for us to impact His world today.

What plans does He have for you this coming year? Whatever they are, you can be sure that He will be with you as you seek to follow Him – as David did.

For prayer and reflection

Lord, I believe you have designed me for Your purposes, and that You will guide and strengthen me in the year ahead as I seek to follow and trust in You. Amen.

ORDER FORM

5 EASY WAYS TO ORDER:

1. Phone in your credit card order: **01252 784710** (Mon–Fri, 9.30am–5pm)
2. Visit our Online Store at **www.cwr.org.uk/store**
3. Send this form together with your payment to:
   CWR, Waverley Abbey House, Waverley Lane, Farnham, Surrey GU9 8EP
4. Visit a Christian bookshop
5. For Australia and New Zealand visit KI Entertainment at **www.cwr4u.net.au**

or a list of our National Distributors, who supply countries outside the UK, visit www.cwr.org.uk/distributors

YOUR DETAILS (REQUIRED FOR ORDERS AND DONATIONS)

Name:	**CWR ID No.** (if known):
Home Address:	
	Postcode:
Telephone No. (for queries):	**Email:**

PUBLICATIONS

TITLE	QTY	PRICE	TOTAL
		Total publications	

All CWR adult Bible-reading notes are also available in ebook and email subscription format.
Visit www.cwr.org.uk for further information.

UK p&p: up to £24.99 = **£2.99**; £25.00 and over = **FREE**

Elsewhere p&p: up to £10 = **£4.95**; £10.01 - £50 = **£6.95**; £50.01 - £99.99 = **£10**; £100 and over = **£30**

Please allow 14 days for delivery   **Total publications and p&p A** | |

SUBSCRIPTIONS* (NON DIRECT DEBIT)

	QTY	PRICE (INCLUDING P&P)			TOTAL
		UK	Europe	Elsewhere	
Every Day with Jesus (1yr, 6 issues)		£15.95	£19.95	Please contact nearest National Distributor or CWR direct	
Large Print *Every Day with Jesus* (1yr, 6 issues)		£15.95	£19.95		
Inspiring Women Every Day (1yr, 6 issues)		£15.95	£19.95		
Life Every Day (Jeff Lucas) (1yr, 6 issues)		£15.95	£19.95		
Cover to Cover Every Day (1yr, 6 issues)		£15.95	£19.95		
Mettle: 14–18s (1yr, 3 issues)		£14.50	£16.60		
YP's: 11–15s (1yr, 6 issues)		£15.95	£19.95		
Topz: 7–11s (1yr, 6 issues)		£15.95	£19.95		
Total Subscriptions (Subscription prices already include postage and packing) **B**					

ease circle which bimonthly issue you would like your subscription to commence from:

AN/FEB MAR/APR MAY/JUN JUL/AUG SEP/OCT NOV/DEC

Only use this section for subscriptions paid for by credit/debit card or
cheque. For Direct Debit subscriptions see overleaf.

CONTINUED OVERLEAF >>

PAYMENT DETAILS

☐ I enclose a cheque/PO made payable to CWR for the amount of: £ _____

☐ Please charge my credit/debit card.

Cardholder's name (in BLOCK CAPITALS) _____

Card No. ☐☐☐☐ ☐☐☐☐ ☐☐☐☐ ☐☐☐☐

Expires end ☐☐ ☐☐

Security Code ☐☐☐

GIFT TO CWR   ☐ Please send me an acknowledgement of my gift   **C** ☐

GIFT AID (YOUR HOME ADDRESS REQUIRED, SEE OVERLEAF)

giftaid it

I am a UK taxpayer and want CWR to reclaim the tax on all my donations for the four years prior to this year **and on** all donations I make from the date of this Gift Aid declaration until further notice.*

Taxpayer's Full Name (PLEASE USE BLOCK CAPITALS) _____

Signature _____ **Date** _____

*I understand I must pay an amount of Income/Capital Gains Tax at least equal to the tax the charity reclaims in the tax year.

GRAND TOTAL (Total of A, B, & C)

SUBSCRIPTIONS BY DIRECT DEBIT (UK BANK ACCOUNT HOLDERS ONLY)

Subscriptions cost £15.95 (except *Mettle*: £14.50) for one year for delivery within the UK. Please tick relevant boxes and fill in the form b

☐ *Every Day with Jesus* (1yr, 6 issues)
☐ Large Print *Every Day with Jesus* (1yr, 6 issues)
☐ *Inspiring Women Every Day* (1yr, 6 issues)
☐ *Life Every Day* (Jeff Lucas) (1yr, 6 issues)

☐ *Cover to Cover Every Day* (1yr, 6 issues)
☐ *Mettle*: 14-18s (1yr, 3 issues)
☐ *YP's*: 11-15s (1yr, 6 issues)
☐ *Topz*: 7-11s (1yr, 6 issues)

Issue to commence f
☐ Jan/Feb ☐ Jul/Aug
☐ Mar/Apr ☐ Sep/Oct
☐ May/Jun ☐ Nov/Dec

CWR

Instruction to your Bank or Building Society to pay by Direct Debit

DIREC Debi

Please fill in the form and send to: CWR, Waverley Abbey House, Waverley Lane, Farnham, Surrey GU9 8EP

Name and full postal address of your Bank or Building Society

To: The Manager _____ Bank/Building Society

Address _____

_____ Postcode _____

Name(s) of Account Holder(s)

☐☐☐☐☐☐☐☐☐☐☐☐☐☐

Branch Sort Code

☐☐ ☐☐ ☐☐

Bank/Building Society account number

☐☐☐☐☐☐☐☐

Originator's Identification Number

4	2	0	4	8	7

Reference

☐☐☐☐☐☐☐☐☐☐☐☐☐☐☐☐☐☐

Instruction to your Bank or Building Society

Please pay CWR Direct Debits from the account detailed in this Instruction su to the safeguards assured by the Direct Debit Guarantee.

I understand that this Instruction may remain with CWR and, if so, details will passed electronically to my Bank/Building Society.

Signature(s) _____

Date _____

Banks and Building Societies may not accept Direct Debit Instructions for some types of account